Bury the Lede

poems by

Maggie Blake Bailey

Finish Line Press
Georgetown, Kentucky

Bury the Lede

ACKNOWLEDGMENTS

"The Moon Rots and Splits" –*Blast Furnace*
"Love Letter" –*Foothill Journal*
"Topography" –*Switchback*
"A Photograph of My Brother, Five Years Old, Jumping into the Pool" –
Rappahannock Review
"I Tried" –*The Southern Poetry Anthology*
"For Carly" –*Town Creek Poetry*
"Arkansas Black" –*Flycatcher: A Journal of Native Imagination*
"Request"– *Slipstream*
"August, Incarnate" –*Tar River*
"Precision" – *Winter Tangerine Review*
"Folly Island" –*Flycatcher: A Journal of Native Imagination*
"Reprieve" –*Heron Tree*
"Bury the Lede" –*Still: The Journal*
"Pavement" –*Amethyst Arsenic*
"Matins for the Poet, Joshua Poteat" –*Heron Tree*
"Arrival" –*Dressing Room Poetry Journal*

Editor: Christen Kincaid

Cover Art: Hannah Dansie

Author Photo: Mary Pendleton Stafford

Cover Design: Elizabeth Maines

Printed in the USA on acid-free paper.
Order online: www.finishinglinepress.com
        also available on amazon.com

Author inquiries and mail orders:
Finishing Line Press
P. O. Box 1626
Georgetown, Kentucky 40324
U. S. A.

Table of Contents

For Andrew. Forever.

The Moon Rots and Splits

We sleep under the pitted light, tucking our knees
into loose flesh, our fingers threaded into cider dark.

The lake at our door flattens, presses its weight
to the bottom and the only movement is mine

and not mine, my unborn daughter kicking against me,
tapping a language I cannot translate.

My body's lexicon no longer concerns me,
my only task is to wait and do no harm.

She flips, tests her new limbs against my walls
and I will myself, *don't bleed, don't bleed, don't bleed.*

This isn't spring, this is autumn. These are not days
to count or squander. No fires burn in our neighbors' yards,

but late wind carries smoke, hints at unseen wreckage.
November waits with yellow hands. I taste the moon,

bitter like medicine. Bitter and alive.

Things to Think, Again
after Bly
for Ryan Sample

Think that someone may bring a bear to your door
and the bear is from Montana, so you are immediately friends,
wants to talk about Tim, the best of your students,
who is a drug dealer now.

Or think that winter, ignored for too long, is seated in your basement,
at the small table set for your red headed daughters,
rising only to make dinner at their miniature stove.

When someone knocks on your door, think that he's
bringing your favorite books, the ones you packed carefully,
think that *Crime and Punishment* is at the top of the stack
and it is a first edition, and you are its author.
Sit down in your chair and write it again.

It's been decided that if you lie down no one will die.
You read that first as a blessing. Now read it as a threat.

Love Letter

One young doe edges the rural highway,
slim muzzle pointed in toward farmland.
The second deer on the distanced edge
turns toward her. Between them,
the stubble of a razed harvest.

A still reservoir, rock hewn and rain cold,
thick brushstrokes of trees, two cranes
pushing sky. As I float in clear water, one fish
bites the mole on my back, small teeth
and the slap of a tail between shoulder blades,
the disappointment of an empty mouth.

Your absence spikes each animal
with need, remakes all movement as
the curtailing of distance, every step forward
a love letter, even, beside the traffic's hum,
the box turtle's shy leather feet on asphalt.

Topography
for Erin Evans

At Lake Oconee, I ask about the depth
and learn that all the lakes of the southeast
more or less are man made: dammed rivers,
ravaged trees standing throat-deep in water,
left for fisheries, the thriving trees on shore
the privacy screens of the wealthy.

As the motor boat skips and slices,
I imagine a cemetery, a schoolyard,
submerged placeholders of a necessarily
abandoned town, the river turning ceilings
into fathoms. The water itself holds
too much silt for us to know. I hear you coughing,

that afternoon on the boat, beers in our hands,
that night on the dock, eating grilled corn,
a bass note, a constant rough and rasped
undercurrent. You say, "I used to only get sick
in the winter." And when we wake up late
on Sunday morning, I am shaking off

the whiskey as you tell me, shyly,
hives have spread to the bottom of your feet.
Timidly you raise your shirt, not for sunscreen
but for me to smooth cream on the welts
that constellate your back, the raised islands
of the topographical and secret map of illness.

I don't tell you about the steeple I pictured
underneath our feet as we swam, scratched
initials in a doorjamb sloughing to driftwood,
backyard gardens of catfish, somnolent, heavy.
I imagine the cough to be a summer cold,
too much pollen, a boat wake against new pilings.

A Photograph of My Brother, Five Years Old, Jumping into the Pool

Arms out, you twist in your leap,
goggles locking on whatever parent
is taking your picture. Unintentional art,
your body breaks planes of sky, ocean, sea
grass. Each wave of turquoise underneath
you mimics the denim, salted blue horizon.

When you come home from war, twenty-five
or so years later, we go for a late drive in the dark
of a post-town suburbia, you talking to me as if
we have always talked and somewhere between
why you love your wife and how our father never
taught you to change a flat tire, you confide,
just this once, that you saw a little girl's face melt off.

You, you are a serious child, a risk taker not
for credit but for action. No *look at me* smile,
instead your mouth is pursed, decided.
I want to say you are so brave. How can I
say I know the truth of you from a photograph
I didn't take on a day I was not even alive.

I Tried

The pull back waste of low tide.
Bait fish racing or left
behind, flipping, silver to sand,
silver to sand, gasping with colder mouths.

Seaweed clings to the shore,
only gains ground in a storm,
hurled a little closer to home.

Doorframe, a lawn mower,
hurricane heaved, thrown
onto the path, taken
by a sea of eel grass.

Even eel grass bent in the wind
with its back turned white,
like bone, white like the crane

at the edge of the tide pool
facing just another crane.

Both, when in flight, resembling arrows.

For Carly

In future memories I am thin.
My poems taste like metal, salt,
a tongue against butterflies pinned
to parchment, old houses after winter.

Feet tucked, I dive arced into swimming
holes I haven't seen. Laughter following
curve, submersion. I wait, underwater,
for language. The slip beneath. And then:

Arms reach across the deeper valley
of my side, a forearm pressed between
my breasts, fingers to clavicle. Dissolve now
against the wholeness of my body.

Bridges Freeze Before Roads

and roads freeze before rivers,
fish fall asleep before birds,
and birds sink before helium,
which freezes last, in a math
known as freezing point
depression, but I'm not sure
how math will save us when

one fawn lies down to sleep
and in the morning, ice holds
hooves, black nose, and thin,
sick haunches to the ground,
marrow red because the body
ate the fat that keeps it white.

Or when a person freezes, sheds
his clothes in an act known as
paradoxical undressing,
one last chance to see cold
as a blessing or an answer.

So when you are hungry
for causation, blame the bridges
for the first tendrils of ice that
kicked the whole world into winter.
Always blame the first to go.

Arkansas Black

If you bite deeply, seeds cut across
white flesh like stars, each a rock
of bewilderment, a brown husk beneath
the tart promise of an Arkansas Black,
sleeve burnished, saved from fermenting
in the bee-thick haze of orchard rows
counting only the simple math of September.

Our back teeth ache in recognition, tongues
trace the first parcel of light branching
into constellations trapped inside our mouths.

Request

I don't care for your glasses. If I didn't
know better, I would think them hipster props,
posed against cardigans, Chuck Taylors, southern
drawl drenched in a Mason jar of whiskey.
Your clothes skirt the edge of cliché,
pull away from your bones like they want
to be sheer, to backlight the width of your hips
when you stand in a window. Lucky shirt,
Jane Kenyon noted, tucked beneath the belt
and the button fly of a man just past the reach
of her hands. But I want where the shirt falls wide,
I want to run one finger down the spokes
of your ribs without soft, interfering fabric.
The gaps are already there, the dismantling begun.

August Incarnate

If it isn't church, it's summer. The ugly
awe of prayer lodged in the blood,
in the throat, in the tongue of hot days.
Catalogue the peripheral words
made flesh in road-kill, in riptide, in light.

Seen this way—

The word of our Lord Jesus Christ pecks
downward at the edge of my vision,
head bobbing, beak thrusting. Buzzard
feathers a rustle of black coins, the glib
metronome face stripping flesh to ribbons.

The word of our Lord Jesus Christ throbs
heavy in an open-eyed dying roadside deer.
Sweet slope to black nose, mouth resting,
peel back of fur, all the ribs tried to hold in:
viscera, heart, nothing that looks like a heart.

The word of our Lord Jesus Christ yields
incandescent yellow, yellow, again, air flash
thick with insect filament, chased and caught,
making momentary lantern panes of childhood
hands. Still storm of light, lightning.

The word of our Lord Jesus Christ breathes
gill-lunged on land: young shark, hook caught
in lower jaw, black smudged fins, shining
like the flesh side of skin, a young boy's
trophy. Sinuous struggle on dock planks.

The word of our Lord Jesus Christ waits
megalithic, tide stranded hump of body
with a letter opener of a tail. Ink blooded,
midnight veined, fossil armored,
slowest crab, horseshoe with no opening.

Seen this way—thanks be to God.

Precision

Name snow rings in the night sky,
rain that cannot hit the ground,
not for metaphor but precision,
say lacuna, meniscus, albedo,
only now, with manure in the air,
only now, at just this height
can the ice gather, say corona,
when you mean wonder: the wrong
words for needing blame, that one
circle of white, held at a distance.

Before the First Snow

comes, the first frost rims
the bay in white, salts
the field, shows the tidal
river course like a vein
on the inside of a wrist.

The ocean demurs in pink,
slate-grey, discards the old
audacious summer blue,
empties the horizon of gulls,
buries clams in black silt.

The wind smells of sap, metal,
groans against the settling house.
The snow that follows drives
slanted, pressing east, collecting
against one wall of each barn,

one face of each jetty, lining
the branches of stunted pines,
doubling the limbs that stretch
into late sky, a second version
stamped in snow. One side waits,

clean and brown, every break
of bark apparent. The other offers
blank submission to winter.
Two versions of the same fury
that sound-proofed the air.

Walking home, looking left,
each pine shows a clean face.
A wooded, living falsehood:
it never snowed, it is only
evening, come a little soon.

Jasper, GA

I rise to feed the wood stove, comforted
by the false blaze of newspaper.
In the morning, the smoke of burnt
ink has rubbed my eyes raw, as if,
in our rough sleep, I read each page to dust.

Over leather-dark coffee, the ranch owner
talks of branding, thieves who travel with thin
irons, ready with a line to turn your mark
to theirs. There is no way to tell, you see,
when the burn was added. Unless you kill
the calf and skin it. On the slick interior,
the new brands flare brighter than old,
flesh without enough time to reconcile
skin to scar. Proof as possession all along.

Folly Island

Canted sunlight punctures Spanish moss:
a hammered tin lantern of late afternoon.

Hawks angle sharp, the nibs of fountain pens,
as whelk shells wear to the last internal spiral.

Morris Island Light crests the bluffs
between teenagers holding bottles, trapping sunset.

None of the starfish are dead enough to take home.
Broken quahogs gleam purple, mauve, a dirty yellow.

My shell greed stutters footprints across
tide lines, while the lighthouse rusts.

Its paint sloughs, littering salt water, the dead panes
counting and recounting old nights crowded with safety.

Reprieve

If you live in good weather long enough
you forget the way light reenters a city,
pulling to its feet the sad ensemble of winter,
shining the grass, spray painting dogwood,
remaking and replacing birds onto boughs.

The days end slowly, requiring no larger
understanding, testing no accomplishment.
The sunlight asks you home and you reply
casually. You are no longer lonely in a city
that seemed built to throw wind down streets,
collect ice in gutters, sidewalks, and pockets.
I bet you don't remember that sense of reprieve:
that gratitude for walking home in the light.

Bury the Lede

When two deer startle
you in the middle of the road
in the middle of the day and then
two blonde boys bounce their ball
at the same point in the road
the next day, duck their heads
and sprint to the sidewalk—

it matters. And when your mother
takes her house off the market,
flirting now with full on bankruptcy,
tells you she does it for you,
and you know the house is a symbol,
but the rot in the basement
distracts you, as does waist high
grass in the yard—

delay the meaning. Instead, wait
for the next deer, this time at dusk
and close enough to press a hand
against the startled flank,
fur stiffer than you expected.

Remember that deer have memories,
whole herds skirt electric fences
that no longer exist, boundaries
that outlive pain. For all the flash
of white tails in headlights, they should
have known better—

defer the impact. Think of the first
time you wanted to leave him,
how you stood barefoot in the kitchen's
stainless dark, only to see a deer
in the yard, both startled eyes open.

Spend your time counting deer. Bury the lede.

The Angel Tells Gideon

You sweat into your grain, slim-waisted
like a girl, hips swaying as you threshed.

I almost never gave you my message,
lost in the brushing of your narrow hand
on your forehead, I almost bent to your wrist-
bones, small like you were small, your profile
cast in tan and gray, burning against blue hills.

You were more a marble than a jewel, more curve
than strength. Your loam-dark eyes, near-sighted.

No matter how many times I flattered the chaff
of your hair, pulled roughly through my fingers,
you made me a thresher just like you.

Gideon Tells The Angel

At first sight you were so unflinchingly
bright, an ache fell through my ribs.

I had been hiding, threshing my heart
into the winepress. I am right to be fearful.

I speak my words and they are stolen,
taken onto horses, driven out of town,

pillaged and plundered. They are the women had.
Precious lost. Crops burned to barrenness.

Given into hands, delivered to the tents
that cannot be counted. Real as locusts.

What good are all your deserts now?
My own father forgets me. And my brother,

who barely smiles, fights the wars.
And you tell me to take out of hands

pressed words, burnt bread, what was loved,
lovely? I am the least of my family.

Pavement

The property belonged to the nearby Magdalen College and the
pavement was discovered in 1910 when alterations were being
made...The pavement was made entirely of the long bones of
oxen...set into the ground. —The Pitt Rivers Museum

A woman remodeled her kitchen
here, and pulled up dirty
toy dirty, food sloppy linoleum.

This being the country I am in
she found bone in the process—

peeled back reluctant checkered squares
and found a pavement of ox bones:
joint bones, leg bones, hollow tunnels,
middle facing up, white against the mortar,
the cobblestones of slaughter, waste,
absence of marrow, laid there even now,
silent under our poorly lit kitchens,
where we pretend our bones are farther
away than what renovations reveal.

Matins for the Poet, Joshua Poteat

Then the rain came,
full of a sadness I had never seen before...

I offer as antidote:

Six sharks, slicing waves to the bone.
        Take each fin as a bookmark, I have worn down
            the sickles with use.

A one-eyed ghost crab, bucking its nocturnality.
        I tricked him into my pocket, and will dance
            him onto your palm, translucent.

The tongue of a knobbed whelk, shy momentary protrusion.
        Pickled in brine to feed, late in the afternoon,
            your unspecified hunger.

Don't say *nothing in the world is ours.*
I am a collector of shells, handful, pocketful,
a reckoning of houses. Listen. The rain has stopped.

Arrival

Last night, leaving a bar in the rain,
I saw a man in a tuxedo

step outside, mount a tandem bicycle,
and ride into a fog-smeared alley.

I know that if I wait long enough,
I'll think in terms of the strange destinations

and promises that lead a man in a tux
to ride a bicycle built for two at midnight:

a girl shivering in a ball gown,
hitching up layers of spun sugar tulle.

An unlikely getaway, a desperate appraisal
of the transportation at hand.

Persistence. Until then, imagine I have
sent him, inexplicably, to your door.

Town Politely Waits for Dead Whale to Explode

I

It's strange what can force a town to wait.
The awkward insistence of a dead whale,
the late night arguments at Patterson's,
old men suggesting dynamite, chainsaws,
funneling gasoline down the blow hole,

and just letting the damn thing burn for days.
All we talk about now is how to erase
what we can't move, can't kill and can't bury.
The priest each Sunday finds new images:
we wait for God like we wait for a whale

to finally explode, or we're the whale
that God is waiting for, but we wonder
how faith could possibly smell like this.
We stop mowing our lawns, tending our rows
of vegetables. What is the point, we ask,

waiting for the sky to rain blubber and guts.
The weeds make the most of our small rebellion.
Our sons think only of water balloons.
Red rubber turning pink against
the strain of tap water, how hard it was

to tie the knot, the burst against a back,
a leg, or shoes. While our golden retrievers
twitch, dreaming of smells that say: *survive*
and you will never go hungry again.

II

Relief smells like an ocean left to rot.
Relief hurts like blood or a heartbeat.

III

The wet kiss of whale meat butchers the clean
white shirts of a Monday morning, wraps veins
like bracelets on arms that meant only to hold
open a door, rolls the hula hoop
slice of an artery past teenagers waiting

for the bus, car alarms announce the slap
of dorsal fins on windshields, and hoods,
as saltwater sluices through gutters,
pushes half eaten krill into the half
hearted creeks that flank the interstate.

IV

Sweeping the fat off the roads takes weeks,
and schools cancel class in the face of rot,
history and math driven out by the stench
of grease and muscle caught in heating ducts,
folds of skin snagged in the slats of benches,
baleen tangled in swings and bicycle spokes.

These days we travel with bleach and tweezers,
wash our sheets again and again each night,
our dinner tables are silent and thick
with the rancid scent of aftermath
under our nails, in our hair, on our tongues.
We have nothing to say to each other now.

V

The rotten heart, still as big as a car,
settles into sand by the boardwalk like
a piece of modern art, and we talk now,
not of chainsaws, anger, and gasoline,
but of pocket knives, stealth, and Tupperware.
We were patient, and we want our relief to last.

Maggie Blake Bailey was born in Maryland and has lived in various states on both coasts. She has degrees from Stanford, Oxford, and Brown Universities and is currently engaged in the School of Letters M.F.A. program at Sewanee, the University of the South. Her poems have appeared in *The Southern Poetry Anthology, Volume V: Georgia, Tar River, Slipstream, The Cider Press Review* and elsewhere. She has twice been nominated for a Pushcart Prize, and *Still: The Journal* nominated the title poem of the collection, "Bury the Lede," for a Best of the Net in 2015. During the year, she teaches English at The Westminster Schools in Atlanta, Georgia, where she lives with her husband and daughter.